EARTHQUAKE REDEMPTION

EARTHQUAKE REDEMPTION
The Seven Seals of Revelation

"The Soon Coming Great End Time Event"

Paul Klumpp

Xulon Press

Xulon Press
2301 Lucien Way #415
Maitland, FL 32751
407.339.4217
www.xulonpress.com

Edited by Xulon Press

Printed in the United States of America.

ISBN-13: 978-1-54561-374-0

CONTENTS

Introduction vii

Part 1   The Lead-In. 1
Part 2   Change of Thought. 7
Part 3   Jesus is Back. 15
Part 4   Be Careful What You Believe 19
        The First Seal
Part 5   Another War, More Mass Killings. . . 29
        The Second Seal
Part 6   Remember The "Good
        Old Days" 33
        The Third Seal
Part 7   Death Without Christ is Hell. 39
        The Fourth Seal
Part 8   The Martyr's Cry 43
        The Fifth Seal
Part 9   No Richter Scale Required 47
        The Sixth Seal
Part 10 Silence is Heard in Heaven. 63
        The Seventh Seal
Part 11 Beyond the Seven Seals of
        Revelation: 67
        The Trumpets
Part 12 Beyond the Seven Seals of
        Revelation: The Bowls 73
Part 13 My Conclusion 77
Part 14 Praying the Will of the Father 81

Bibliography. 91
About the Author 93

Introduction

The Book of Revelation is one of the most mysterious and controversial books of the Bible. I have read a number of books and studies about the book of Revelation and they all seem to focus on events in the distant future—not where we are living right now and the days just ahead.

It has been implied that all the events in Revelation relating to the seals, the trumpets, and the vials are going to start happening after the antichrist signs a peace treaty with Israel, which starts the "Great Tribulation", (7 years of horrible events) but what force or event will bring this signing to pass? When are these end-time events going to happen? Then someone reminds me that we are now living in the end-times. Do you think so? I do!

The end of time, right on! That must surely be why there are so many abortions, shootings, suicides, rapes, beatings, bombings, and killings. What is the message in all of these grim, evil, sick, and ungodly events of our day? Or does all the evil and corruption say something about where we are and what is soon to come next, living now in the last days?

The book of Revelation is not about events in the future anymore, for we are living in the Bible future, the final chapter. We have lived in this period since Jesus Christ returned to heaven to retake His seat at the right hand of God in the throne room where the Heavenly

Father had patiently been waiting for His Son's return from earth. We read in Revelation 5:7 *"Then He (Jesus) came and took the scroll out of the right hand of Him (God) who sat on the throne"*. As soon as Jesus returned to heaven, His Father handed Him a book that was inscribed within and sealed with seven seals. It says in Revelation 5:9 that no other man anywhere was worthy to open the seals, except Jesus Christ.

> *"and they sang a new song, saying:*
> *"You are worthy to take the scroll,*
> *And to open its seals;*
> *For You were slain,*
> *And have redeemed us to God by*
> *Your blood*
> *Out of every tribe and tongue*
> *and people and nation""*

Jesus immediately opened the first four seals and released the riders (angels) on their horses to go to the earth and carry out what they were assigned and given power to do. The first four angels (known as The Four Horsemen) that were released are: Deception, War, Hunger, and Death (and Hell). The work of these four released angels has been ongoing and intensifying every day for almost 2,000 years since they were released on the population of planet earth.

I believe the fifth seal has also been opened, but not yet fulfilled. This is where we are living now: in the time span of the fifth seal. It deals with Christian martyrs and it bears a condition before it can be fulfilled (or stoped). Read Revelation 6:11b: *"Then a white robe was given to each of them (the martyrs); and it was said to them that they should rest a little while longer, until both the number of their fellow servants and their brethren, who would be killed as they were, was completed."*

So when the number of martyrs who die for the cause of Christ is fulfilled, then will come the opening of the sixth seal and when it is opened, every person alive on planet earth will know it has been opened and what it represents, so be ready. This short book has been prepared to help all who read it, to know where the whole human race is living in the final countdown towards the end of time.

If you are a non-believer, then you may not read past this introduction, but I pray you will read on and accept Jesus Christ into your heart by asking him to forgive you of all your sins, to wash you clean with His shed blood, and then ask Him to be your Savior and your Lord for the rest of your life, however long that may be. Read 2 Corinthians 5:17: *"Therefore, if anyone is in Christ he is a new creation: Old things have passed away; behold, all things have become new";* so start reading the Bible and the Holy Spirit will teach you and lead you each day of your new life in Him.

If you are a believer in Jesus Christ, then read about where we are presently living in the book of Revelation and ask the Holy Spirit to awaken your spirit to the joyful task of winning souls for Jesus for whatever time remains. For the joy of the Lord is your strength. Read in Nehemiah 8:10: *Then he said to them, "Go your way, eat the fat, drink the sweet, and send portions to those for whom nothing is prepared; for this day is holy to our Lord. Do not sorrow, for the joy of the LORD IS YOUR STRENGTH."* Rejoice and look up, for your redemption draws near.

I have purposely tried to keep this book short and to the point so you can read it quickly and if needed, pray for forgiveness, get right with God, and be ready for the opening of the sixth seal.

Part 1

The Lead-In

The Book of Revelation, the last book of the Bible; I must have read it through more than sixty times over the past forty years, but never seeming to gain a clear understanding of what it was saying to me. In my heart, I felt that eventually the Holy Spirit would give me an understanding of at least some of the scriptures, so I continued to read.

The one thing I did understand from Revelation was a day would come when God would shut down everything on earth and judge every person according to their works, but that did not satisfy me, so I continued to read.

In October of 2002, I was on a two-week business trip in the State of Washington. It was Saturday afternoon on October 12th, and I was in my motel room reading the headline story in Friday's *USA TODAY* newspaper about the sniper shootings in Maryland, Virginia, and Washington, D.C.

In September 2001, there was the destruction of the World Trade Center in New York City, and now these senseless killings thirteen months later, I sat and thought about the killing of innocent people. I thought about end-time events and tried to figure if these two current events somehow fit together.

I laid the newspaper down and closed my eyes, and asked God about 9/11 and now this new event. What did it all mean? God responded quickly to my question. He immediately told me to get my Bible and open it to Ezekiel 21, which was titled in my Bible, "Babylon, the Sword of God." After reading the chapter, I thought to myself, *What am I supposed to get from the thirty-two verses I read?* Then the Lord broke in and said to me, "Now go back and read again verses one through seven," which I did and it read:

> *[1]And the word of the Lord came to me, saying, [2]"Son of man, set your face toward Jerusalem, preach against the holy places, and prophesy against the land of Israel; [3]and say to the land of Israel, 'Thus says the Lord: "Behold, I am against you, and I will draw My sword out of its sheath and cut off both righteous and wicked from you. [4]Because I will cut off both righteous and wicked from you, therefore My sword shall go out of its sheath against all flesh from south to north, [5]that all flesh may know that I, the Lord, have drawn My sword out of its sheath; it shall not return anymore."' [6]Sigh therefore, son of man, with a breaking heart, and sigh with bitterness before their eyes. [7]And it shall be when they say to you, 'Why are you sighing?' that you shall answer, 'Because of the news; when it comes, every heart will melt, all hands will be*

2

*feeble, every spirit will faint, and all
knees will be weak as water. Behold, it
is coming and shall be brought to pass,'
says the Lord God."*

"Now read it again," He said, "but this time when you
read the name 'Jerusalem,' change it to 'New York
City' and when you read the name 'Israel,' change it
to 'America'":

"And the word of the Lord came to
me, saying, "Son of man, set your face
toward [New York City], preach against
the holy places, and prophesy against
the land of [America]; and say to the
land of [America], 'Thus says the Lord:
'Behold, I am against you, and I will
draw My sword out of its sheath and cut
off both righteous and wicked from you.
Because I will cut off both righteous and
wicked from you, therefore My sword
shall go out of its sheath against all
flesh from south to north, that all flesh
may know that I, the Lord, have drawn
My sword out of its sheath; it shall not
return anymore.' Sigh therefore, son of
man, with a breaking heart, and sigh
with bitterness before their eyes. And
it shall be when they say to you, 'Why
are you sighing?' that you shall answer,
'Because of the news; when it comes,
every heart will melt, all hands will be
feeble, every spirit will faint, and all

knees will be weak as water. Behold, it
is coming and shall be brought to pass,'
says the Lord God."

So I reread the seven verses again as instructed, and the
Holy Spirit said to me that God was sick of the pungent
odor of sin rising up from America—a foul stench. It
is the only nation that prints on their currency, "In God
We Trust," but the statement is an abomination unto
God. I saw the message in the changed verses, God's
Judgement.

The Lord went on to say "There are four sins in particular that have created this foul stench in my nostrils
and they are: abortion, greed, gay rights, and total dis-
regard for My day of rest and worship (Sunday)." The
Lord said He would no longer turn and look away from
America's sinful lifestyle that they had chosen.

God said His wrath would be revealed in various
ways and not only on America, because the whole world
has chosen to live in the garbage dump of sin. God's
wrath is revealed to man as a warning of His displeasure
from His heart of love. It's like a loving dad who has
to punish his son for his disrespect and disobedience.
Usually it hurts the dad more than the son, but in different parts of the body. God the Father and His Word
(the Bible) declare punishment is justified to restore
respect and order, both in the home and on earth. Look
at the American society today where physical punishment has been outlawed. Today we can see the results
of disrespect toward God and what it has created; no
respect and no order and many people feel that's the
way life was meant to be, until one of their children dies
from a gunshot wound to the head from some unknown,

smart-alecky kid who said a friend dared him to do it. Today there are young children in their homes who plot and scheme against their God-given parents.

What has happened to parents who taught Godly respect and order in the home? The Supreme Court judges said the methods to achieve honor and respect should be outlawed. God's Word clearly states in Proverbs 13:24, *"He who spares his rod hates his son, but he who loves him disciplines him promptly."*

Receiving God's wrath is neither fun nor pleasant. How it is received depends largely on the hearts of the recipients and how it's received also reveals one's relationship with God the Father. God's wrath can be viewed as a wakeup call to a person, a group, or a nation of people. This was observed in the USA after 9/11; churches were full, but it didn't last long.

The various events that have occurred over the past sixteen years have been a warning that few people on planet earth have recognized or heeded. The heart of man is hard and unyielding. Our loving God said in His Word (The Bible) in 2 Chronicles 7:14: *"If My people who are called by My name will humble themselves, and pray and seek My face, and turn from their wicked ways, then I will hear from Heaven, and will forgive their sin and heal their land."* This is a clear explanation as to how to improve life on earth but it is plain to see that very few really want a change.

The Lord also said in Isaiah 55:6-7 through His prophet: *6"Seek the Lord while He may be found, call upon Him while He is near.7Let the wicked forsake his way, and the unrighteous man his thoughts; let him return to the Lord, and He will have mercy on him; and to our God, for He will abundantly pardon."*

Then hear what God says in Lamentations 3:32: *"Though He causes grief, yet He will show compassion according to the multitude of His mercies."*

Out of the seven verses that I reread in Ezekiel 21, there were two verses in particular that the Holy Spirit burned into my heart and they were verses six and seven. From the New King James Version, they read:

> [6] *"Sigh therefore son of man, with a breaking heart, and sigh with bitterness before their eyes. [7] And it shall be when they say to you, 'Why are you sighing?' that you shall answer, 'because of the news when it comes, every heart will melt, all hands will be feeble, every spirit will faint, and all knees will be weak as water. Behold it is coming and shall be brought to pass,'" says the Lord God.*

I wondered what kind of an event would produce that kind of reaction from people who do not care. What would it be? Something financial, detonation of dirty bombs, meteor shower, collision with an asteroid, a solar storm, what?

I thought to myself, *if the question arose from reading the Bible, then the answer would come from reading the Bible.* So I began to read and search for the answer. I felt this possibly could be some "end-time event," so one more time, I opened my Bible to the book of Revelation.

Part 2

Change of Thought

Several years have passed and I have continued to read the book of Revelation through several more times along with Daniel, Ezekiel, Jeremiah, and Matthew and the entire Bible chronologically, but still no real breakthrough as to what the book of Revelation said about "now" other than the end is coming and the events of the seven seals, the seven trumpets, and the seven vials are clearly stated in Revelation 6, 8, 9, 11, and 16.

At some time in mid-2009, a friend of mine, Dr. Gary D. Smith, gave me a book titled *Earthquake Resurrection* by David W. Lowe (Bibliography #3). My eyes caught the smaller print on the cover written under the bold title, which stated "Supernatural Catalyst for the Coming Global Catastrophe." To me, this statement sounded interesting, but even so, at the time I was reading the Bible through chronologically as a thorough study and did not want to pause for anything, so I put David Lowe's book aside to read later.

Later, in February 2010, I picked up David Lowe's book and I noticed it was a first edition printed in 2005, so I felt the information would be both current and relevant. As I read through the book, I found it interesting; then I came to Chapter 7, titled "The Sixth Seal of the

Scroll: Global Catastrophe." I realized several things from reading this chapter, but the main thing I realized was the first five seals have already been opened by Jesus Christ. The first four were opened shortly after His return to heaven. The fifth seal related to martyrs, was opened I think sometime later but the conditions of the fifth seal are not yet fulfilled. The sixth and seventh seals have not yet been opened.

Then I realized when the sixth seal is opened, this earth-shaking event would be so terrible, it became clear to me, this is the event that will make *"every heart melt, all hands feeble, every spirit faint, and all knees weak as water"*. Ezekiel 21:7: *[7] And it shall be when they say to you, 'Why are you sighing?' that you shall answer, 'Because of the news; when it comes, every heart will melt, all hands will be feeble, every spirit will faint, and all knees will be weak as water. Behold, it is coming and shall be brought to pass,' says the Lord GOD."* This is the next biblical Revelation event that will occur within the next few years, probably sooner than most would like to think and this is based on world events of our days and time.

Let's look at where we are concerning the book of Revelation. Every Christian knows Jesus Christ is God's only begotten Son and was born to Joseph and Mary by a supernatural conception of God; as we read in Matthew 1:18-25: *[18] Now the birth of Jesus Christ was as follows: After His mother Mary was betrothed to Joseph, before they came together, she was found with child of the Holy Spirit. [19] Then Joseph her husband, being a just man, and not wanting to make her a public example, was minded to put her away secretly. [20] But while he thought about these things, behold, an*

8

angel of the Lord appeared to him in a dream, saying, "Joseph, son of David, do not be afraid to take to you Mary your wife, for that which is conceived in her is of the Holy Spirit. [21] And she will bring forth a Son, and you shall call His name Jesus, for He will save His people from their sins."

[22] So all this was done that it might be fulfilled which was spoken by the Lord through the prophet, saying: [23] "Behold, the virgin shall be with child, and bear a Son, and they shall call His name Immanuel," which is translated, "God with us."

[24] Then Joseph, being aroused from sleep, did as the angel of the Lord commanded him and took to him his wife, [25] and did not know her till she had brought forth her firstborn Son.[a] And he called His name Jesus."

And in Luke 1:26-31: *"[26]And in the sixth month the angel Gabriel was sent from God unto a city of Galilee, named Nazareth, [27]To a virgin espoused to a man whose name was Joseph, of the house of David; and the virgin's name [was] Mary. [28]And the angel came in unto her, and said, Hail, [thou that art] highly favoured, the Lord [is] with thee: blessed [art] thou among women. [29]And when she saw [him], she was troubled at his saying, and cast in her mind what manner of salutation this should be. [30]And the angel said unto her, Fear not, Mary: for thou hast found favour with God. [31]And, behold, thou shalt conceive in thy womb, and bring forth a son, and shalt call his name JESUS."*

As prophecy had proclaimed, Mary was a virgin and gave birth to Jesus. Read in Isaiah 7:14: *[14] Therefore the Lord Himself will give you a sign: Behold, the virgin shall conceive and bear a Son, and shall call His name Immanuel."* The Bible tells us that Jesus grew up to

9

be a sinless man. (Hebrews 4:15: *"¹⁵ For we do not have a High Priest who cannot sympathize with our weaknesses, but was in all points tempted as we are, yet without sin."*). Jesus became a High Priest in the order of Melchizedek (Luke 3:23: ***"The Genealogy of Jesus Christ*** *²³ Now Jesus Himself began His ministry at about thirty years of age,"* and in Hebrews 5:10: *"¹⁰ called by God as High Priest "according to the order of Melchizedek,"*). We read when He started His ministry He selected twelve disciples and taught them about the love of God and the power in living a righteous life (Matthew 10:1-4: ***"The Twelve Apostles.*** *¹And when He had called His twelve disciples to Him, He gave them power over unclean spirits, to cast them out, and to heal all kinds of sickness and all kinds of disease. ² Now the names of the twelve apostles are these: first, Simon, who is called Peter, and Andrew his brother; James the son of Zebedee, and John his brother; ³ Philip and Bartholomew; Thomas and Matthew the tax collector; James the son of Alphaeus, and Lebbaeus, whose surname was Thaddaeus; ⁴ Simon the Cananite, and Judas Iscariot, who also betrayed Him."*). Then Jesus died on a cross as a sinless sacrifice (The Lamb of God) for all the sins of mankind; (Mark 15:27-28: *²⁷ With Him they also crucified two robbers, one on His right and the other on His left. ²⁸ So the Scripture was fulfilled which says, "And He was numbered with the transgressors."*). and he rose again on the third day. So now through the shed blood of Jesus Christ, we can ask for and receive forgiveness from all our sins, both past and present. (Romans 5:6-11: ***Christ in Our Place*** *⁶ For when we were still without strength, in due time Christ died for the ungodly. ⁷ For scarcely for a righteous* *man will one die; yet perhaps for a good man someone would even dare to die. ⁸ But God demonstrates His own love toward us, in that while we were still sinners, Christ died for us. ⁹ Much more then, having now been justified by His blood, we shall be saved from wrath through Him. ¹⁰ For if when we were enemies we were reconciled to God through the death of His Son, much more, having been reconciled, we shall be saved by His life. ¹¹ And not only that, but we also rejoice in God through our Lord Jesus Christ, through whom we have now received the reconciliation.")*. Then we become a new creation in Christ; old things will pass away and we will live in newness of life in Christ (2 Corinthians 5:17: *¹⁷ Therefore, if anyone is in Christ, he is a new creation; old things have passed away; behold, all things have become new.")*. By reading and studying the Bible, praying, fellowshipping with other believers, and always being sensitive to the Holy Spirit (John 14:26 *²⁶ "But the Helper, the Holy Spirit, whom the Father will send in My name, He will teach you all things, and bring to your remembrance all things that I said to you."*) (John 16:13: *¹³ "However when the Spirit of Truth has come, He will guide you into all truth."*) (John 8:12: *¹² Then Jesus spoke to them again, saying, "I am the light of the world. He who follows Me shall not walk in darkness, but have the light of life."*)

We can walk as Christ walked, talk as Christ talked, and think as Christ thought, as living examples of Jesus Christ, God's only begotten Son. Now we can be counted among the righteous and receive eternal life in heaven when our life on earth comes to an end. Thank you Jesus.

After Jesus Christ was sacrificed on the cross as we read in the Bible, He was properly buried in a borrowed tomb (Isaiah 53:9: *⁹ And they made His grave with the wicked— But with the rich at His death, Because He had done no violence, Nor was any deceit in His mouth."*; Matthew 27:57-60: ***Jesus Buried in Joseph's Tomb*** *⁵⁷ Now when evening had come, there came a rich man from Arimathea, named Joseph, who himself had also become a disciple of Jesus. ⁵⁸ This man went to Pilate and asked for the body of Jesus. Then Pilate commanded the body to be given to him. ⁵⁹ When Joseph had taken the body, he wrapped it in a clean linen cloth, ⁶⁰ and laid it in his new tomb which he had hewn out of the rock; and he rolled a large stone against the door of the tomb, and departed."*); according to prophecy and He rose again on the third day (Mark 16:6: *⁶ But he* (an angel) *said to them, "Do not be alarmed. You seek Jesus of Nazareth, who was crucified. He is risen! He is not here. See the place where they laid Him."*), as He said He would. He fellowshipped with His disciples and many others for a period of forty days after His resurrection, as read in 1 Corinthians 15:6: *"After that, he was seen by over five-hundred brethren at once; of whom the greater part remain to the present, but some have fallen asleep."*

Then he led His disciples out to a desired location (Bethany) where He told them to continue to preach and teach all He had taught to them and He commanded them to wait for the "Promise of the Father," as read in Acts 1:4: *"And, being assembled together with them, He (Jesus) commanded them not to depart from Jerusalem, but to wait for the Promise of the Father."* Also, in Acts 1:9-11: **Jesus Ascends to Heaven** *⁹ "Now when He had* *spoken these things, while they watched, He was taken up, and a Cloud received Him out of their sight. [10]And while they looked steadfastly toward heaven as He went up, behold, two men stood by them in white apparel," [11]who also said, "Men of Galilee, Why are you standing here looking up into Heaven? This same Jesus which you saw rising up into Heaven will come again in the same way that you saw Him go into Heaven."*

So as we read about Jesus leaving His disciples, He leaves earth to return to heaven (Mark 16:19: *"So then, after the Lord had spoken to them, He was received up into Heaven, and sat down at the right hand of God."*) Also, in Luke 24:51: *"Now it came to pass, while He blessed them, that He was parted from them and carried up into Heaven."* Lastly, Acts 1:9: *"Now when He had spoken these things, while they watched, He was taken up, and a cloud received Him out of their sight,"* and it continues in Mark 16:19b: *"He was received up into Heaven and sat down at the right hand of God."*

Part 3

Jesus is Back

So Jesus left the earth and His disciples to go back to heaven and be seated again on His throne at the right hand of God, His Father. We read in Revelation 5 how John is shown the Throne Room of Heaven and it says in verses one and two: *¹And I saw in the right hand of Him who sat on the throne a scroll written inside and on the back, sealed with seven seals. ²Then I saw a strong angel proclaiming with a loud voice, "Who is worthy to open the scroll and to loose its seals?"*

John realized there was no man in heaven or on the earth or under the earth who was worthy to open the seals. I think all Christians would agree Jesus is the only man who is worthy, so where is Jesus at this time? We know from scripture that the throne of Jesus was at the right hand of God, but obviously Jesus was not present in heaven, otherwise John would have seen Him. The Bible also states there was no one on earth who came forth to open the seals; so, where is Jesus?

As I paraphrased what Mr. David Lowe implied in his book in Chapter 11, the clear answer to the where abouts of Jesus, is that the scene at the opening of Revelation 5 does not take place in John's future. John is looking back in time. In the vision that was being shown, Jesus had not yet arrived in Heaven's Throne

Room, but was still ascending up from earth and just before He arrived in Heaven to take His seat at the right hand of God. It clearly says in Revelation 5:2: *"Then I saw a strong angel proclaiming with a loud voice, 'Who is worthy to open the scroll'?"* This is a vision of the scene in God's Throne Room just after Jesus was lifted up from earth *"to loose the seals? And no one in heaven or on earth or under the earth was able to open the scroll or look at it."*

I believe John wept because he expected to see Jesus step up and take the scroll and open it, but that didn't happen. In Rev. 5:5, it says as John bitterly wept *"But one of the elders came to him and said: Do not weep. Behold, the Lion of the tribe of Judah, the Root of David has prevailed to open the scroll and to loose its seven seals"*

Then, reading on, in Rev 5:6-7:

> [6] *"And I looked, and behold, in the midst of the throne and of the four living creatures, and in the midst of the elders, stood a Lamb as though it had been slain, having seven horns and seven eyes, which are the seven Spirits of God sent out into all the earth. [7] Then He came and took the scroll out of the right hand of Him who sat on the throne."*

So Jesus is now present with God and immediately He went to His Father and took the scroll out of the right hand of God.

From Revelation 5: 8-10, we read:

> [8]*"Now when he had taken the scroll, the four living creatures and the twenty-four elders fell down before the Lamb, each having a harp, and golden bowls full of incense, which are the prayers of the saints [9]And they sang a new song, saying: 'You are worthy to take the scroll, and to open its seals; for You were slain, and have redeemed us to God by Your blood out of every tribe and tongue and people and nation, [10]and have made us kings and priests to our God; and we shall reign on the Earth".*

Then John watched as Jesus opened the first seal. I believe the opening of the first seal happened within the first few moments after Jesus arrived in heaven. Jesus knew exactly what He was to do when He arrived and it appears God held the scroll in His right hand, as He waited for Jesus to arrive. Read in Revelation 5:7: *"Then He came and took the scroll out of the right hand of Him who sat on the throne."*

Now let's look at each individual seal and see what destruction and hardship comes from the opening of each one.

Part 4

Be Careful What You Believe

THE FIRST SEAL

Before we talk about the individual seals, allow me to make a few general comments about the "seven seals." Seals one to four and six involve actions toward people living on the earth. The fifth and seven seals take place in heaven. The first five seals have already been opened and are still in progress today. Each person who has ever lived since the opening of the first seal has had a choice as to the total impact and effect of the open seals on their lives.

I believe from reading the scriptures that Jesus opened the first five seals soon after His return to heaven. The first four seals (sometimes phrased as the "Four Horsemen") represent four individual spirits that were released on the earth to carry out their specific assignment on the people of earth from that time and will continue their individual works until the Trumpets are sounded. The intensity of evil of these four released spirits (opened seals) has intensified every day from the time of their release (about A.D. 33) until now (2018) which is about two thousand years. The opening of the seventh seal by Jesus is Christ is documented by John in Rev. 8: 1-2: ***Seventh Seal: Prelude to the seven Trumpets*** *[1] "When He opened the seventh seal, there was silence in heaven for about half an hour. [2] And I saw the seven angels who stand before God, and to them were given seven trumpets."*

And also in Revelation 6:1-17:

First Seal *(The Deceiver): Revelation 6:1-2*

> *[1]Now I saw when the Lamb opened one of the seals; and I heard one of the four living creatures saying with a voice like thunder, "Come and see." [2]And I looked, and behold, a white horse. He who sat on it had a bow; and a crown was given to him, and he went out conquering and to conquer.*

Second Seal *(War): Revelation 6:3-4*

> *[3]When He opened the second seal, I heard the second living creature saying, "Come and see." [4]Another horse, fiery red, went out. And it was granted to the one who sat on it to take peace from the Earth, and that people should kill one another; and there was given to him a great sword.*

Third Seal *(Hunger and Starvation): Revelation 6:5-6*

[5]When He opened the third seal, I heard the third living creature say, "Come and see." So I looked, and behold, a black horse, and he who sat on it had a pair of scales in his hand. [6]And I heard a voice in the midst of the four living creatures saying, "A quart of wheat for a denarius, and three quarts of barley for a denarius; and do not harm the oil and the wine."

Fourth Seal *(Ongoing Death on Earth): Revelation 6:7-8*

[7]When He opened the fourth seal, I heard the voice of the fourth living creature saying, "Come and see." [8]So I looked, and behold, a pale horse. And the name of him who sat on it was Death, and Hades followed with him. And power was given to them over a fourth of the earth, to kill with sword, with hunger, with death, and by the beasts of the earth.

Fifth Seal *(The Cry of the Martyrs): Revelation 6:9-11*

[9]When He opened the fifth seal, I saw under the altar the souls of those who had been slain for the word of God and for the testimony which they held. [10]And they cried with a loud voice, saying, "How long, O Lord, holy and true, until You judge and avenge our blood on

*those who dwell on the earth?" [11]Then a white robe was given to each of them; and it was said to them that they should rest a little while longer, until both the number of their fellow servants and their brethren, **who would be killed as they were**, was completed.*

Sixth Seal *(A Great Shaking of Earth): Revelation 6:12-17*

[12]I looked when He opened the sixth seal, and behold, there was a great earthquake; and the sun became black as sackcloth of hair, and the moon became like blood. [13]And the stars of heaven fell to the earth, as a fig tree drops its late figs when it is shaken by a mighty wind. [14]Then the sky receded as a scroll when it is rolled up, and every mountain and island was moved out of its place. [15]And the kings of the earth, the great men, the rich men, the commanders, the mighty men, every slave and every free man, hid themselves in the caves and in the rocks of the mountains, [16]and said to the mountains and rocks, "Fall on us and hide us from the face of Him who sits on the throne and from the wrath of the Lamb! [17]For the great day of His wrath has come, and who is able to stand?"

The blood of the martyrs I believe is being avenged.

Seventh Seal *(Silence in Heaven):* Revelation 8:1

> *¹When He opened the seventh seal, there was silence in heaven for about half an hour."*

Now looking back, the first seal is opened and described in Revelation 6:1-2:

> **First Seal: The Conqueror:** *¹ Now I saw when the Lamb opened one of the seals; and I heard one of the four living creatures saying with a voice like thunder, "Come and see." ² And I looked, and behold, a white horse. He who sat on it had a bow; and a crown was given to him, and he went out conquering and to conquer."*

John looked and saw a "white horse;" the rider of the horse is a spirit or angel who was released on the earth. Let's look at the rider to see what his given authority will do. He who sat on the "white horse" had a bow and a crown was given to him and he went out conquering (deceiving) and to conquer. This is interesting: we see a rider on a "white horse" who is given a crown, but let's look for a moment at the real thing in Revelation 19:11-13:

Christ on a White Horse *¹¹ Now I saw heaven opened, and behold, a white horse. And He who sat on him was called Faithful and True, and in righteousness He judges and makes war. ¹² His eyes were like a flame of fire, and on His head were many crowns. He*

had a name written that no one knew except Himself.
[13] He was clothed with a robe dipped in blood, and His name is called The Word of God. (See John 1:14: *And the Word became flesh and dwelt among us*).

Now looking back, what does John see in Revelation 6:1-2? He sees a deceiver, an imitator, an imposter, a rider on a white horse with a crown and carrying a bow, his weapon. However, Christ in Revelation 19 rides a "white horse" with many crowns on His head and His weapon is in His mouth: it's a sharp two-edged sword, His Word.

Revelation 19:1-21: ***Heaven Exults over Babylon***
[1] After these things I heard a loud voice of a great multitude in heaven, saying, "Alleluia! Salvation and glory and honor and power belong to the Lord our God! [2] For true and righteous are His judgments, because He has judged the great harlot who corrupted the earth with her fornication; and He has avenged on her the blood of His servants shed by her." [3] Again they said, "Alleluia! Her smoke rises up forever and ever!" [4] And the twenty-four elders and the four living creatures fell down and worshiped God who sat on the throne, saying, "Amen! Alleluia!" [5] Then a voice came from the throne, saying, "Praise our God, all you His servants and those who fear Him, both small and great!"

[6] And I heard, as it were, the voice of a great multitude, as the sound of many waters and as the sound of mighty thundering, saying, "Alleluia! For the Lord God Omnipotent reigns! [7] Let us be glad and rejoice and give Him glory, for the marriage of the Lamb has come, and His wife has made herself ready." [8] And to her it was granted to be arrayed in fine linen, clean and bright, for the fine linen is the righteous acts of the saints.

⁹ *Then he said to me, "Write: 'Blessed are those who are called to the marriage supper of the Lamb!'" And he said to me, "These are the true sayings of God."* ¹⁰ *And I fell at his feet to worship him. But he said to me, "See that you do not do that! I am your fellow servant, and of your brethren who have the testimony of Jesus. Worship God! For the testimony of Jesus is the spirit of prophecy."*

Christ on a White Horse ¹¹ *Now I saw heaven opened, and behold, a white horse. And He who sat on him was called Faithful and True, and in righteousness He judges and makes war.* ¹² *His eyes were like a flame of fire, and on His head were many crowns. He had a name written that no one knew except Himself.* ¹³ *He was clothed with a robe dipped in blood, and His name is called The Word of God.* ¹⁴ *And the armies in heaven, clothed in fine linen, white and clean, followed Him on white horses.* ¹⁵ *Now out of His mouth goes a sharp sword, that with it He should strike the nations. And He Himself will rule them with a rod of iron. He Himself treads the winepress of the fierceness and wrath of Almighty God.* ¹⁶ *And He has on His robe and on His thigh a name written: KING OF KINGS AND LORD OF LORDS.*

The Beast and His Armies Defeated ¹⁷ *Then I saw an angel standing in the sun; and he cried with a loud voice, saying to all the birds that fly in the midst of heaven, "Come and gather together for the supper of the great God,* ¹⁸ *that you may eat the flesh of kings, the flesh of captains, the flesh of mighty men, the flesh of horses and of those who sit on them, and the flesh of all people, free and slave, both small and great."*

[19] And I saw the beast, the kings of the earth, and their armies, gathered together to make war against Him who sat on the horse and against His army. [20] Then the beast was captured, and with him the false prophet who worked signs in his presence, by which he deceived those who received the mark of the beast and those who worshiped his image. These two were cast alive into the lake of fire burning with brimstone. [21] And the rest were killed with the sword which proceeded from the mouth of Him who sat on the horse. And all the birds were filled with their flesh."

Again the first rider (spirit/angel) John saw on a white horse must be identified as an imposter or to be more exact a deceiver of the truth who was immediately released upon the earth to do his work with his bow, to shoot fiery darts of deception and lies into the hearts of believers, going forth conquering their souls and forever to conquer until Jesus comes back to earth.

Now, let's go back to Matthew 24:3-5: **The Signs of the Times and the End of the Age** *[3] Now as He (Jesus) sat on the Mount of Olives, the disciples came to Him privately, saying, "Tell us, when will these things be? And what will be the sign of Your coming, and of the end of the age?" [4] And Jesus answered and said to them: "Take heed that no one deceives you. [5] For many will come in My name, saying, 'I am the Christ,' and will deceive many."* (will conquer their souls).

We don't see a lot of people running around saying they are the Christ, (a recent National Geographic article identifies six alive today, with followers) but we do see many pastors (false teachers) standing behind their pulpits preaching a false gospel, deceiving millions and millions of people.

Matthew 24:11 says, *"Then many false prophets will rise up and deceive many."* Read what Jesus said in answering the question His disciples asked Him. The question was, "What shall be the sign of thy coming, and of the end of the age?" Jesus's answer did not speak of various "end-time" tragic events; what He said was, Matthew 24:4 "take heed that no one deceives you." So the first major sign of the coming end is a time of "great deception" and if you haven't noticed, "we have arrived."

Speaking of this day and time, it says in 2 Timothy 3:13, *"but evil men and impostors will grow worse and worse, deceiving and being deceived."*

Isn't it ironic that the first spirit (angel) released on the earth came riding on a white horse with a crown, a spirit of deception, and he has had almost two thousand years to shoot his fiery darts of lies into the hearts and lives of men, women, boys, and girls? Today people have been deceived so much that they call wrong, "right," and right, "wrong." This lying, deceiving spirit is more active today and growing stronger with each passing day and the proof is in front of our faces in the daily newspaper, the internet, TV, politicians, lying pastors, and global business leaders.

Jesus said in John 14:6, "I am the way, the truth, and the life." In this day and time, be careful what you believe, but know this: there is only one truth and one way to the Father and that is through Jesus Christ, God's only Son, the Lamb of God, who takes away the sin of the world.

Part 5

Another War, More Killing

THE SECOND SEAL

Deception and lies are only the beginning. Let's look back at John's vision: he sees Jesus open the second seal. It says in Revelation 6:3-4: *³"When he opened the second seal, I heard the second living creature saying "come and see." ⁴Another horse, fiery red, went out. And it was granted to the one who sat on it to take peace from the earth, and that people should kill one another; and there was given to him a great sword.*

John looked and saw another horse; this one was red and it said the rider of the red horse was given the authority to take peace from the earth, causing nations to make war and kill one another in mass.

Killing of people in mass is not something new. In the Old Testament, there are records of one army going out and killing another army of nearly 80,000 soldiers. But the wars of the Old Testament were of a spiritual nature where God used armies to bring judgement on a nation of people either killing the opponent or to bring them into captivity. Looking at international battles and religious wars fought since A.D. 300 through the Second Congo War in 2003 in which about five million died, it is estimated that more than two billion people have been killed in or because of wars fought since the rider was released after the second seal was opened. Now as we read on in Revelation 6:4: *"⁴ Another horse, fiery red, went out. And it was granted to the one who sat on it to take peace from the earth, and that people should kill one another; and there was given to him a great sword."* The rider of the red horse was given power to take peace from the earth and they should make war and kill one another (in battle). The verse goes on to say the "spirit of war" was given a great sword (or weapon). We will come back later and explain what the great sword is about.

Now remember the effects or works of the released spirits do not happen all at once. Each spirit did begin his work immediately upon reaching the earth, but the impact or the effect has been gradual but is continuously getting worse with time, like a cancer. Today, in 2017, we can easily see the results of life on earth without peace. Every believer should know that Jesus is the peace giver (The Prince of Peace) and so if any living person wants to have real peace, the only way to obtain it is through Jesus Christ, the "Prince of Peace." See John 14:27: *"Peace I leave with you, My peace I give to you; not as the world gives do I give to you. Let not your heart be troubled, neither let it be afraid."*

Also in John 16:33: *"These things I have spoken to you, that in Me you may have peace. In the world you will have tribulation; but be of good cheer, I have overcome the world."*

Read Romans 8:6: *"For to be carnally minded is death, but to be spiritually minded is life and peace."*

Additionally, Romans 14:17: *"For the kingdom of God is not eating and drinking, but righteousness and peace and joy in the Holy Spirit."*

Romans 15:33: *"Now the God of peace be with you all. Amen."*

1 Corinthians 1:3: *"Grace to you and peace from God our Father and the Lord Jesus Christ."*

2 Corinthians 13:11: *"Finally, brethren, farewell. Become complete. Be of good comfort, be of one mind, live in peace; and the God of love and peace will be with you."*

Philippians 4:7: *"And the peace of God, which surpasses all understanding, will guard your hearts and minds through Christ Jesus."*

Lastly, Philippians 1:2: *"Grace to you, and peace, from God our Father, and from the Lord Jesus Christ."*

The fighting of wars has been continual since peace was removed from the earth and the weapons of war have been continually developed and evolved from sling-shots, swords, bow and arrows, and spears. Until what came along to end World War II, the Manhattan Project during the 1930s was the forging of the Great Sword, a weapon of mass destruction (WMD) that was used on the people of Japan not once, but twice, to end World War II.

The "Great Sword" that was referred to in Revelation 6:4: (*"[4] Another horse, fiery red, went out. And it was granted to the one who sat on it to take peace from the earth, and that people should kill one another; and there was given to him a great sword."*) that the rider was given, I believe referred to the atomic bomb, i.e. nuclear weapons, which at present are the greatest single weapon known to man.

If you recall in Matthew 24:6: Jesus said in His discussion about end-time events, "*⁶ And you will hear of wars and rumors of wars. See that you are not troubled; for all these things must come to pass, but the end is not yet.*"

Each day in the news, there is information given about wars being fought somewhere on the planet, but the end is not yet.

Part 6

Remember the "Good Old Days"

THE THIRD SEAL

Now John sees Jesus open the third seal and he looked and saw a rider on a black horse. He stated in Revelation 6:5: *"When He opened the third seal, I heard the third living creature say, 'Come and see.' So I looked, and behold, a black horse, and he who sat on it had a pair of scales in his hand."*

We see a spirit (angel) that is released on the earth to cause poverty, starvation, and a major shortage of food (if you could find it for sale; it would cost a lot).

In 2014, wheat prices rose seventy-seven percent and rice sixteen percent; these were some of the sharpest rises in food prices, ever. However, in 2015, the speed of change has accelerated. "Since January, rice prices have soared 141 percent; the price of a variety of wheat shot up twenty-five percent in one day. The era of cheap food is over. The transition to a new equilibrium is proving costlier, more prolonged, and much more painful than anyone had expected" (quoted from *The Economist*, "The New Face of Hunger," 9-28-15).

The shortage of food generates massive starvation, which already is a worldwide problem today and each day it only gets worse. The shortage of food has escalated over the past thirty years or so. China presently is buying or leasing large pieces of land on any continent, where they can grow needed crops for their people of over one billion. China does not want a reoccurence of the great famine in 1959 to 1961 that killed an estimated 34 million people.

Between climate changes, insects, plant diseases, and a worldwide population quickly approaching eight billion people who want to eat every day, the food supply and quality are decreasing and the cost is currently increasing with each growing season. So depending on where you live and how much money you have, your next meal could be your last. The black horse rider (the angel of starvation) continues his work, affecting the lives of most people on planet earth.

I personally grew up in "The Good Old Days", a day and time when there was plenty of good, wholesome, fresh, domestically grown farm produce. You could consume the food without fear of dying, or deforming your unborn child. This was a time before Organic. Now if food is not stamped "Organic" you consume it at your own risk. Organic has raised the price more.

Today, we eat food such as canned goods, frozen food, so-called fresh meats, seafood, farm produce, dairy products, and it is all to some degree contaminated with chemicals or insecticies or bacteria, but we as Americans feel safe because we know that all foods consumed by us are inspected and are then declared safe for consumption. Right?

On the other hand, we no longer can safely consume fish or shrimp from the Pacific Ocean because of an unfortunate nuclear power plant incident in Japan.

We think we are blessed far beyond those who do not have enough food to eat and yet we die early deaths because of deadly toxins we consume day after day. I think often of the "Good Old Days" that are long gone.

I personally was exposed to a situation that impacted my thinking about starving, hungry people in America. A few years ago on my first trip to Washington, D.C., I was on The Mall when, outside one of the buildings around 12:30pm, I noticed a man, rather unkempt, who was bent over and digging in a garbage can on the sidewalk. I paused for a moment in shock and observed. He then straightened up with an item in each hand. In his right hand, he had a half-eaten banana and in the other hand, he held what looked like a piece of fried chicken. Then he appeared pleased with his findings and began consuming them as he walked off to check another garbage can.

I watched for a moment more as he approached another garbage can. There was a security officer nearby and when the man began to dig into the can contents, the officer made him leave.

I thought, *how ironic; here I am, in the nation's capital with all of its many fine restaurants, affluent politicians, and elaborate museums, and here is a man who survives by consuming partially-eaten food out of garbage cans.*

God then reminded me this scene is only one of millions played out each day in the U.S. and it represents a nation of people who have chosen to serve other gods and not remembering the words of God as stated in

Proverbs 14:34: *"Righteousness exalts a nation, but sin is a reproach to any people."*

God also said in all of His love in 2 Chronicles 7:14: *"If My people, who are called by My name will humble themselves, and pray and seek My face, and turn from their wicked ways, then I will hear from Heaven, and will forgive their sin and heal their land."*

We don't want to do things right; we say we have a better way and yet as God's Word says, it's so easy to do it His way.

Another piece of information I found that vividly shows how bad off the whole world is. It said on the Internet every four seconds, someone dies of starvation (that is 21,600 people each day or 7,884,000 per year). Everyone has heard the old saying, "America throws away enough food everyday to feed all the starving people in the world."

Food shortage is a tragic reality that is with us now and is only going to get worse with each passing day. There are several forces that are beyond man's knowledge and ability that play a big part in the growth and harvest of food crops that we put in our mouths each day.

Some good news to help offset some of the current bad news relating to the demise of food crops is taken from an article titled, "How We'll Grow Food In The Future" from *Popular Science*, 9-22-15, by Kevin Gray. It talks about vertical farming and its many great advantages, like it requires ninety-five percent less water and no sunlight. The article also spoke of controlled techniques to mass cultivate shrimp and other sources of seafood (aquaculture), and using modern technology to collect data from fields to improve agricultural yields to feed the hungry.

It will be a few years before the pluses start to over-take the negatives. In the meantime, every Christian believer needs to pray and to be thankful for the abundance that we Americans presently have each mealtime. We should look hard for ways to share our abundance with those less fortunate.

It would be something if churches in various countries of the world (mainly the U.S.) would change the elaborate construction of their buildings and use the money to feed the starving hungry masses.

Jesus said in Matthew 26:11: *"For you have the poor with you always."* So you would think the church's leaders would believe the scriptures and be sure they provide always for the poor around the world. Helping people in need should be a major effort of the church of today.

Part 7

Death Without Christ is Hell

THE FOURTH SEAL

Again, John looked and saw Jesus (Revelation 6:7-8: *Fourth Seal: Widespread Death on Earth* *⁷ When He opened the fourth seal, I heard the voice of the fourth living creature saying, "Come and see." ⁸ So I looked, and behold, a pale horse. And the name of him who sat on it was Death, and Hades followed with him. And power was given to them over a fourth of the earth, to kill with sword, with hunger, with death, and by the beasts of the earth."*)

Notice there are two riders on the pale horse. The first rider was Death and sitting behind Death was Hades (Hell). Power was given unto them by God to kill people on one-quarter of the earth (See Reference Information at the end of Part 7) using weapons (guns, knives), natural disasters (storms, earthquakes, tsunamis), sickness, starvation, and with beast-of-the-earth (poison snakes, lions, bears). Here is an interesting fact: the land surface of the main continents of the earth (excluding Antarctica) equals right at one-fourth of the total surface of the planet; so now we see whom these spirits will target with their power to kill mankind. We all have witnessed the results of their power from the opening of the fourth seal to our present time and they have been very active.

Think for a moment of some of the natural disasters that have occurred over the past fifty years or so. Earthquakes: China – 1976, Haiti – 2010, Indonesia – 2004, over 750,000 people were killed in these three events. To add to these are tsunamis, droughts, famines, floods, plagues (Ebola, The Black Death, polio), and murders (which includes abortions) all over the world where millions and millions have been killed and these killings will continue to increase until Jesus Christ comes back to earth. Come quickly, Lord Jesus.

By the way, the "death or killing spirit" has no respect for anyone. He will kill your children, your mother, your sister, your brother, and anyone else, any day, anytime, anywhere (high school, college, movie theater, church, or outside your own house). At this time in the world, the spirit of "death" is doing his thing, unchecked, for more than 151 thousand deaths each day.

So, in summary we see the first four seals (spirits or angels) that were opened (released) by Jesus Christ upon His arrival back to heaven were released to help all mankind make a choice and "choose this day whom you will serve" according to Joshua 24:15: *"¹⁵ And if it seems evil to you to serve the LORD, CHOOSE FOR YOUR-SELVES THIS DAY WHOM YOU WILL SERVE, WHETHER THE GODS WHICH YOUR FATHERS SERVED THAT WERE ON THE OTHER SIDE OF THE RIVER, OR THE GODS OF THE AMORITES, IN WHOSE LAND YOU DWELL. BUT AS FOR ME AND MY HOUSE, WE WILL SERVE THE LORD."*

The dead can no longer change their choice; we all make our choices while we live, so think about it, who or what is your God? You may want to reconsider your choice and choose eternal life in Jesus Christ. In these last days, the scripture says *"that whoever calls on the name of the Lord shall be saved."* (Acts 2:21)

As the destructive influence of each of these four spirits has intensified over the past two thousand years, people alive today make choices concerning the things that will determine and influence their eternal destiny. Most people do not understand they are choosing heaven or hell. They do not see where they are or where they are going. They are blinded to the light of the truth (Jesus is the light of the world and He is the only truth). The four spirits are so subtle in what they do and they have been doing it for so long in front of us that we accept their activity as normal and tell one another, "Have a nice day."

REFERENCE INFORMATION

Total Area of the Earth: 196.9*
Total Area of the Oceans: <u>139.7*</u>
Total Area of the Land: 57.2*
Exclude Antarctica: 5.4*
Mountains & Lakes &
Water Ways & Desserts   <u>2.57*</u>
                           49.2* or 25%

*million square miles

Part 8

The Martyrs' Cry

THE FIFTH SEAL

Revelation 6:9 says the fifth seal is opened and reveals a scene in the Throne Room of Heaven where John writes: *"When He (Jesus) opened the Fifth Seal, I saw under the Altar (of God), the souls of those who had been slain for the word of God and for their testimony, which they (the martyrs) held."* Revelation 12:11 says, *"And they overcame him (Satan) by the Blood of the Lamb and by the word of their testimony, and they did not love their lives to the death."*

In Revelation 6:10, these martyrs are crying out to God with a loud voice saying: *"How long, O Lord, holy and true, until You judge and avenge our blood on those who dwell on the Earth?"* It was said to them: *"That they should rest a little while longer, until both the number of their fellow servants and their brethren, who would be killed as they were, was completed."*

So this is a holding point in the opening of the sixth seal.

I am uncertain as to the day and time in which the number of martyrs will be completed or fulfilled. It will be soon. There are Christians in this world who die for their beliefs and testimony of the Word of God as martyrs every day. Even most recently in the state of Oregon, at Umpqua Community College, nine more martyrs were added to God's uncompleted number. When the heaven known count of martyrs is completed on planet earth and God says, "That's it, the count is finished," then Jesus will take the book and open the sixth seal. I feel God's "chosen number or count of martyrs" is soon to be completed or fulfilled, so be prepared for the greatest shaking the world has ever known.

Make sure you are righteous and holy in the sight of God before the opening of the sixth seal because God will require every believer's services in the days after the shake, as explained in the next chapter.

It is interesting to note that in the verses of Revelation 6: 9 -11, the word "martyrs" is defined but not used. The biblical definition as stated in Revelation 6: 9, *as those who had been slain for the word of God and for the testimony which they held*.

An additional notation: the word "martyr" (singular) is only used twice in the Bible in Acts 22:20 (*[20] And when the blood of Your martyr Stephen was shed, I also was standing by consenting to his death, and guarding the clothes of those who were killing him.*" [speaking of Steven] and Revelation 2:13 (*[13] "I know your works, and where you dwell, where Satan's throne is. And you hold fast to My name, and did not deny My faith even in the days in which Antipas was My faithful martyr, who was killed among you, where Satan dwells.*") where Jesus is speaking about "the compromising church and he mentions the name of Antipas as His faithful martyr.

The word "martyrs" (plural) is only used once in the entirety of the Bible in Revelation 17:6 (*[6] I saw the woman, drunk with the blood of the saints and with the blood of the martyrs of Jesus. And when I saw her, I marveled with great amazement."*) where a statement is given about "the blood of the martyrs of Jesus".

Part 9

No Richter Scale Required

THE SIXTH SEAL

The opening of the sixth seal is dramatized by a great shaking of the entire planet, which has never happened before. The human mind cannot begin to imagine the severity of this mighty shaking event.

Please take note of the major difference about the opening of the sixth seal as compared to the opening of the first five seals. Everyone alive on the planet will know the instant that the sixth seal is opened because of the catastrophic event that they will witness. If they know nothing about the sixth seal event, they may think it is only a most terrible local earthquake, if they live through its devastation. Globally, millions could die during this short earth-shaking event, but on the other hand the few days following this event, millions will be born-again, come to know and accept Jesus Christ as their personal Savior and Lord. Hallelujah!

We have all seen on YouTube, TV news, newspapers, or first-hand the terrible destructive power delivered by a strong earthquake on a city's buildings and structures. Can you imagine what a 15 or 16 magnitude shake of the whole planet would do in a twenty or thirty second period? I think we would all have trouble imagining the massive destruction that would result.

Let's take a close look at what John the Revelator said in Revelation 6:12-17 about the sixth seal:

> [12] *I looked when He opened the sixth seal, and behold, there was a great earthquake; and the sun became black as sackcloth of hair, and the moon became like blood.* [13] *And the stars of Heaven fell to the earth, as a fig tree drops its late figs when it is shaken by a mighty wind.* [14] *Then the sky receded as a scroll when it is rolled up, and every mountain and island was moved out of its place.* [15]*And the kings of the earth, the great men, the rich men, the commanders, the mighty men, every slave and every free man, hid themselves in the caves and in the rocks of the mountains,* [16]*and said to the mountains and rocks, "Fall on us and hide us from the face of Him who sits on the throne and from the wrath of the Lamb!* [17]*For the great day of His wrath has come, and who is able to stand?"*

First, take note, there is more said about the sixth seal than any other seal. Second, this is the only seal opened that has a direct, immediate impact on every person alive on the planet and that everyone will clearly recognize and understand that this event is God's wrath released on mankind (see verses 15-17). Also, this event will satisfy the cry of the martyrs who ask, *"How long, O Lord, holy and true, until You judge and avenge our blood on those who dwell on the earth?"* (Revelation 6:10-11).

The response to the martyrs was, "they should rest a little while longer."

Now let's carefully consider the event statements of the opened sixth seal. Jesus opens the sixth seal and there was a great earthquake (Revelation 6:12 ***Sixth Seal: Cosmic Disturbances*** *[12] I looked when He opened the sixth seal, and behold, there was a great earthquake; and the sun became black as sackcloth of hair, and the moon became like blood."*). Now keep in mind that John is trying to describe this twenty-first century future event as best as he can with his first century understanding. John used the words "great earthquake," for what he witnessed, to describe the violent shaking of the whole earth. As I understand, an earthquake is a local shifting of two (or more) of the earth's plates along a fault line and depending on the pressure on the two plates and the amount of movement, the destructive damage can be great or small, depending on how close to the epicenter manmade structures are located.

The violent shaking of the whole earth that John witnessed was so strong it set off a chain reaction of other destructive events. Notice what is said next in verse 12: *"the sun became black."* This is because the great shaking breaks the earth's crust in numerous places and volcano-type eruptions immediately begin to erupt all over the world producing thick smoke and ash.

It goes on to say *"the heaven rolled together like a scroll."* This is the result of volcanic ash and smoke filling the sky and shutting out the sun. This has been witnessed in local areas when volcanoes have erupted; the smoke and ash shut out the sun. Many of us remember the massive amount of ash that was dumped into the sky when Mount St. Helens erupted in the state of Washington in 1980.

Let's look again at the imagined destructive results from the great shake of the entire planet. The earth's surface or crust will buckle everywhere. All roads, building foundations, the great Pyramids of Egypt, the Dome of the Rock in Jerusalem, and most all other buildings will collapse, along with communication towers and highway tunnels will cave in. Most prisons, college dorms, and hospitals will be destroyed along with the world's super-highways and all airport run-aways. This means all airplanes in flight will not have a safe place to land. Did you know it is estimated that at any given point in time the average number of people in-flight is approximately 500,000?

From the results of the great shake, most of the structures we know of and see everyday will be destroyed, most types of communication that we know and use will no longer work, millions of people will be killed, both good and bad. Most real Christians (the true believers in the Lord Jesus Christ) will supernaturally be kept alive, because they immediately will be inspired to rise up out of the chaos and rubble and will go forth into their local areas, anointed by God, to be a living miracle working power and witness of the Lord Jesus Christ. More on this later.

Revelation 6:13 says John saw the stars of heaven fall unto the earth (*[13] And the stars of heaven fell to the earth, as a fig tree drops its late figs when it is shaken by a mighty wind."*).

Now we all know the blazing objects John saw falling out of the sky were not stars. So what did John see falling that he identified as stars with his understanding? This was most likely a meteor shower, or the shower of burning objects was a raining down of satellites and space debris that has been left in orbit (20,000 pieces documented). Because all communication structures will be destroyed from the great shaking of the planet, guidance signals will be lost and these guided objects would spin out of control, crashing into other pieces and adding to the display of pieces raining down upon the earth. Another thing that comes to mind is to see burning objects falling through earth's atmosphere, there needs to be a dark backdrop, which is generally provided by the dark side of the earth. Possibly what is being said here is all the earth's surface is dark due to the smoke and ash that fills the earth's atmosphere. The display of objects falling from the sky could be clearly seen by John due to the gross darkness that prevailed.

Please keep in mind that the great earthquake spoken of in Revelation 6:12 is a violent shaking of the whole earth, more violent than our minds can imagine. So not only will all communications, as we know it—cell phones, radios, television, shortwave—be interrupted, but so will other services that we depend on, such as: electricity, natural gas, water, sewage, and garbage pickup. This will instantly affect all homes, apartments, schools, hospitals, businesses, and airports that may have parts left intact. For additional scientific explanation of soon coming earthquakes and a colder earth, read the newly published book by John L. Casey entitled "Upheaval" (Bibliography #2). Pay close attention to chapter 8, page 148 to 185. He has a great deal to say about life after a major earthquake. We both agree that staying alive after the shake and keeping ones family safe is going to be a major struggle.

If you own a gasoline-powered generator, it will serve you (if you have something electrical that still works) until you need to go buy more gasoline. Remember, you will not be able to buy anything on credit, all electricity will be off and you can only walk to where you need to go. This is the way it will be for several weeks or months: no roads, no electricity, no communication, and a sunless sky filled with volcanic ash and smoke making it difficult to breathe and to see.

Homes and commercial buildings that were designed and built to code for seismic activity requirements will not hold up during this great earth shake.

Pay attention and make note of everything you see the next time you drive anywhere; most of everything you see will be destroyed, including the road you are traveling on.

I hope the horror of what is left after the great shaking that results from the opening of the sixth seal is becoming more clear. If you are a non-believer left alive and able-bodied after the shaking event, then life will be extremely tough and primitive for the next few months.

Remember, due to the volcanic ash and smoke in the sky that will blacken the sun, it will be difficult to breathe and to move about in the darkness. The only outside source of light and heat will come from fires generated from gas leaks, burning homes and auto wrecks. After days of no sunlight, the surface temperature will drop and become cold and this will add to the overall discomfort and hopelessness.

If you doubt that the global shaking will be as powerful as I have tried to describe it, look at what the Bible says in Revelation 6:14b: *"Every mountain and island was moved out of its place."* It says *every* mountain and island will be relocated. That will take a powerful global shaking force to relocate the position of every mountain and every island on the earth. The mountains will also partially crumble during the shaking.

Out of the devastating global disaster, God showed me that His mercy endures forever in Psalm 118:29, *"Oh, give thanks to the Lord, for He is good! For His mercy endures forever."*

The Lord showed me that He is preparing a great host of true, born-again believers who have an eye to see and an ear to hear what the Holy Spirit is revealing and saying to His body: So I proclaim to every believer to watch, be prepared, for the day is coming when God will call you to come forth for service. For during this time of great global destruction, God will protect and safeguard those spirit-filled believers. After the shaking has stopped, these righteous individuals will immediately rise up with a special anointing of God's power through His great love to go forth and do mighty works in Jesus' Name. Great miracles will be done by these believers through the laying on of hands and speaking faith in the power of Jesus' name. Through this period of five or six days (non-stop) after the great shake, the greatest harvest of souls will be won to the Kingdom of God that has ever been known to man, millions and millions of people all over the world will be "born-again" and accept Jesus Christ as their Savior and Lord. This will be the last Great Spiritual Revival on planet Earth.

A great display of God's Mercy that endures forever, as clearly stated in Psalms 136:1-26:

Thanksgiving to God for His Enduring Mercy
[1] "Oh, give thanks to the Lord, for He is good! For His mercy endures forever. [2] Oh, give thanks to the God of gods! For His mercy endures forever. [3] Oh, give thanks to the Lord of lords! For His mercy endures forever: [4] To Him who alone does great wonders, For His mercy endures forever; [5] To Him who by wisdom made the heavens, For His mercy endures forever; [6] To Him who laid out the earth above the waters, For His mercy endures forever; [7] To Him who made great lights, For His mercy endures forever. [8] The sun to rule by day, For His mercy endures forever; [9] The moon and stars to rule by night, For His mercy endures forever. [10] To Him who struck Egypt in their firstborn, For His mercy endures forever; [11] And brought out Israel from among them, For His mercy endures forever; [12] With a strong hand, and with an outstretched arm, For His mercy endures forever; [13] To Him who divided the Red Sea in two, For His mercy endures forever; [14] And made Israel pass through the midst of it, For His mercy endures forever; [15] But overthrew Pharaoh and his army in the Red Sea, For His mercy endures forever; [16] To Him who led His people through the wilderness, For His mercy endures forever; [17] To Him who struck down great kings, For His mercy endures forever; [18] And slew famous kings, For His mercy endures forever, [19] Sihon king of the Amorites, For His mercy endures forever; [20] And Og king of Bashan, For His mercy endures forever. [21] And gave their land as a heritage, For His mercy endures forever; [22] A heritage to Israel His servant, For His mercy endures forever. [23] Who remembered us in

our lowly state, For His mercy endures forever; [24] And rescued us from our enemies, For His mercy endures forever; [25] Who gives food to all flesh, For His mercy endures forever. [26] Oh, give thanks to the God of heaven! For His mercy endures forever."

After a short period of five or six days, sinful men's hearts will become cold and hard, selfish and greedy and sinful ways will again take control and dominate day-to-day living and the old game of "king of the mountain" will be reenacted until military rule is established around the world, in the main populated areas.

I believe it is possible, God will snatch away all believers from the earth, six to eight days after the great shaking because there will be a point in time, maybe six to eight weeks after the shake that no civil person will be safe. There will be a "kill or be killed" attitude and a "what's yours is mine" philosophy where anything goes. The man with the biggest gun and the most ammunition will live and take whatever he wants. God help the man trying to protect his family during this period of time.

Let's look now at something so special the Lord showed me: more of what is going to happen during the Great Shake. The God-given land of Israel will be kept completely safe during the Great Shake. Not one brick of a Jewish or Christian home (or business) in all of Israel will be shaken. The Lord showed me the twentieth century drawing of Jews back to Israel was because it is their homeland that God Almighty gave to them forever. In more recent years, God has drawn them back home for their own safekeeping. I was so excited when the Holy Spirit showed me that all Jews in Israel would be kept safe along with their possessions. This protection is also extended to all Christian believers living inside the "original borders" of Israel.

I believe Israel's safe-keeping by God will be a powerful witness and sign to all Arabs in the Middle East and will in time bring to pass the signing of a peace treaty with the surrounding Arab countries. This action will usher in the beginning of Daniel's seventieth week; see Daniel 9:27: *"Then he (the anti-Christ) shall confirm a covenant (treaty) with many for one week (a week represents a period of seven years), but in the middle of the week (three and a half years), he (the Antichrist) shall bring an end to sacrifice and offering. And on the wing of abominations shall be one who makes desolate, even until the consummation, which is determined, is poured out on the desolate."*

This is when a suave, diplomatic businessman will represent the Arab countries and confirm a covenant (or peace treaty) with the Jews for a period of seven years.

As was mentioned previously, the great shake will not affect anything Jewish within the original God-given borders of Israel (The Promised Land). Now this brings up an interesting point: is there anyone alive today (or historical records) who could mark off the true God-given border or boundaries that God gave to the Children of Israel? All those who know God's Word know the original land God gave to the Jews (the twelve tribes) which was "The Promised Land" is several times larger than the present-day borders of the state of Israel. This original land will be the bordered land that God will protect and guard over for every Jew and their possessions within these borders. Any dwelling, properties and possessions of non-Jews or non-Christians within the original borders will be destroyed; this includes the "Dome of the Rock" and all other Muslim mosques. (Now the new Jewish Temple can be quickly constructed on the original temple site).

The peace treaty or covenant of Daniel's seventieth week is for a period of seven years. At the start of this seven-year period, the Jews will immediately begin construction of a new Jewish temple, which I believe will be written into the wording of the peace treaty. It will most likely take just a few months to construct the new temple and immediately upon its completion, the Orthodox Jews will begin offering up animal sacrifices unto God as they did in the Old Testament times. The priests are already trained and waiting. We know sacrificial offerings will be done because in Daniel 9:27a it says: *"Then he shall confirm a covenant with many for one week; but in the middle of the week He shall bring an end to sacrifice and offering."*

Then he (the antichrist) shall confirm a covenant (peace treaty) with many for one week (seven years), but in the middle of the week (three and one half years from signing) the antichrist shall bring an end to sacrifice and offering in the Temple. He will take over the temple and bring to pass the abomination of desolation spoken of by Daniel the Prophet in Daniel 12:11: *"And from the time that the daily sacrifice is taken away, and the abomination of desolation is set up, there shall be one thousand two hundred and ninety days"* (3 ½ years).

Let's go back and look at Revelation 6:15-17 to look at man's reaction to the devastation of the Great Shaking of planet Earth. It says: *[15] And the kings of the earth, the great men, the rich men, the commanders, the mighty men, every slave and every free man, hid themselves in the caves and in the rocks of the mountains, [16] and said to the mountains and rocks, "Fall on us and hide us from the face of Him who sits on the throne and from the wrath of the Lamb! [17] For the great day of His wrath has come, and who is able to stand?"*

What these verses tell me is all sinful men who are still alive on the earth will have a clear understanding that the wrath of Jesus Christ (the Lamb) has been poured out on the earth, but more importantly they show sinful man realizes staying alive is going to be extremely hard. What a powerful opportunity this offers for every Christian alive to rise up at the call of God and go forth into the devastated community where people are hurting and afraid and to freely pour out the healing power of God's love unto salvation.

What the Holy Spirit showed me about the five or six days following the great shake is: if you are a righteous, spirit-filled, Jesus-loving individual, then you and all those in your house will be kept safe, including your physical home and your possessions (even your animals). You will continue to have electric power and other essentials such as gas, water, and sewage, but those around you who are not believers, will lose everything—in some cases, even their lives, but God through you will restore their lives. You will be given authority over death and injuries to God's glory.

Now, here is more good news for God's righteous! If you, as a spirit-filled believer, have any sickness, ailment, pain, or disability you have been living with, in your body, the moment that the shake occurs, you will be healed and made whole, at that instant, no matter what was wrong with you. You will feel a powerful anointing come over you and the Holy Spirit will immediately empower you to go out into your community and begin to share love, healing, health, and life to those in need, through the name of Jesus.

This means you will, by God's power, put arms back on a person, you will heal broken necks and backs, restore crushed skulls, raise the dead, and whatever else needs to be done to reveal the power of God's love to all unbelievers so their souls may be won to Christ. You will be empowered to go non-stop, twenty-four hours a day for whatever number of days is given for the harvest of souls for the Kingdom of God. Every believer on the planet will be empowered to go out immediately and minister to the lost who are hurting, dying, dead, hungry, and ready to listen, knowing God's wrath has turned their world upside down.

Keep in mind: you will only be able to go out and move about by the power and leading of the Lord. Outside, it will be dark all over the world. The air will be filled with smoke and ash; there will be no warmth radiating from the sun. Hopefully you will have extra food, water, and blankets to share as you move through the many homes in your neighborhood sharing the power of God's love and recovery with the lost and broken.

For the entire world, this will be the last great harvest of souls and hundreds of millions will come to know Christ, as the believers glean the fields that are white unto harvest. Don't forget to pray for the other laborers you have won to Christ so they may go forth winning even more to Jesus Christ during this short period of time.

Each believer should start now to prepare spiritually for the events that will happen at the opening of the sixth seal, which is going to happen sooner than any of us think, so get ready.

As the period of intense ministry continues for every believer who is obeying the direction and leading of the Holy Spirit, what is going to happen next?

The earth at this time is a mess, the "great shake" has destroyed almost every structure built by man. Volcanoes have filled the sky with thick ash and smoke has blocked the sun and the earth's temperature is dropping. There is twenty-four-hour darkness, but the love of Christ flowing out of believers will be warmth and light that will draw men like a moth to a flame. Remember: the harvest will only last a few days, because the heart of sinful man will begin to quickly harden and he will begin to focus his attention and strength on his own personal needs and wants. A spirit of selfishness, greed, anger, and killing will quickly consume the fleshly heart of man and killings will become commonplace. I believe it is during the start of this period that God will rapture His church.

We know all civilizations will be hit hard by the "great shake," but life on planet Earth does settle down and the masses regroup, the air clears somewhat, and the path of man leads to Daniel's seventieth week, the seven years of great tribulation, which the opening of the seventh seal ushers in.

I am uncertain as to how much time passes by from the opening of the sixth seal to the opening of the seventh seal. It could be eighteen to twenty four months during which a worldwide, aggressive rebuilding program will happen.

Remember, the Jewish people in Israel do not have to rebuild and God reestablished the true border of Israel. Every structure within the true border of Israel that was not Jewish or Christian was destroyed and the

Jews will be busy cleaning all the foreign rubble out of the way for new construction, such as a new tabernacle built on the original temple site. As I understand, the new Jewish temple is already designed and built, waiting to be constructed in its rightful place.

There is very little hope for sinful man after the great shake of planet Earth, except in Jesus Christ. Without Christ, life will be worthless, and the next event is the rapture (a snatching away) of all Christians who are still alive after the great shake.

Part 10

Silence Heard in Heaven

THE SEVENTH SEAL

The opening of the seventh seal by Jesus, as viewed and documented by John in Revelation 8:1-6:

Seventh Seal: Prelude to the Seven Trumpets ¹*When He opened the seventh seal, there was silence in heaven for about half an hour.* ²*And I saw the seven angels who stand before God, and to them were given seven trumpets.* ³*Then another angel, having a golden censer, came and stood at the altar. He was given much incense, that he should offer it with the prayers of all the saints upon the golden altar which was before the throne.* ⁴*And the smoke of the incense, with the prayers of the saints, ascended before God from the angel's hand.* ⁵*Then the angel took the censer, filled it with fire from the altar, and threw it to the earth. And there were noises, thunderings, lightnings, and an earthquake (shaking).* ⁶*So the seven*

angels who had the seven trumpets pre-
pared themselves to sound.

Verse one tells us immediately, when the seal was opened, there was silence in heaven for about half an hour. What a contrast from the opening of the sixth seal.

I am uncertain as to the significance of the thirty minutes of silence in heaven, unless it is heaven's way of showing remorse for what is to be soon released upon the sinful people remaining on planet Earth. As the old saying goes, "all hell will soon be released."

In verse two, John says he saw seven angels standing before God and each of them was given a trumpet. Then in verse six, it says the seven angels who had the seven trumpets prepared themselves to blow their trumpets.

I believe the blowing of the first trumpet is the beginning of Daniel's seventieth week or the seven years of the Great Tribulation, which closes with the "Battle of Armageddon" and the return of Jesus Christ to planet Earth to start His one thousand-year reign of peace and love.

Mankind who remains alive on the planet at the blowing of the trumpets are basically on their own. You can see where it clearly states man's heart is hardened and he will not repent: in Revelation 9:20-21: *"[20] But the rest of mankind, who were not killed by these plagues, did not repent of the works of their hands, that they should not worship demons, and idols of gold, silver, brass, stone, and wood, which can neither see nor hear nor walk. [21] And they did not repent of their murders or their sorceries or their sexual immorality or their thefts."*

This concludes the word that I heard from the Holy Spirit concerning the "Seven Seals of revelation". The question that comes out of all this information is: when will the "Sixth Seal" be opened? Matthew 24:36: *36 "But of that day and hour no one knows, not even the angels of heaven, but My Father only"*. Matthew 24:44: *"44 Therefore you also be ready, for the Son of Man is coming at an hour you do not expect."*

The Holy Spirit impressed on me that the time is coming soon, for the great shake event, so everyone needs to be ready. Come quickly, Lord Jesus, come quickly.

Now lets look ahead at the coming events after the great shake and the "rapture", to see what those who remain alive on the earth can expect. The period is called "The Great Tribulation" (for seven years) which begins shortly after the opening of the Seventh Seal, "Silence in Heaven".

This seven year period is a most horrible period of time on the earth called "The Great Tribulation" which is composed of "The seven Trumpets" and "The Seven Viles" (Bowls) climaxing with "The Battle of Armageddon", the final battle between good and evil. Next comes the thousand year Reign with Christ on earth.

Part 11

The Trumpets

Read what is in store for the remaining population of earth during the blowing of the seven trumpets in Revelation 8:7-13, 9:1-21 and 11:15-19

First Trumpet: *Vegetation Struck (Revelation 8:7)*

> *[7]"The first angel sounded: And hail and fire followed, mingled with blood, and they were thrown to the earth. And a third of the trees were burned up, and all green grass was burned up."*

Second Trumpet: *The Seas Struck (Revelation 8: 8-9)*

> *[8]"Then the second angel sounded: and something like a great mountain burning with fire was thrown into the sea, and a third of the sea became blood. [9] And a third of the living creatures in the sea died, and a third of the ships were destroyed."*

Third Trumpet: *The Waters Struck (Revelation 8:10-11)*

[10] *"**Then the third angel sounded:** And a great star fell from heaven, burning like a torch, and it fell on a third of the rivers and on the springs of water. [11]The name of the star is Wormwood. A third of the waters became wormwood, and many men died from the water, because it was made bitter."*

Fourth Trumpet: *The Heavens Struck (Revelation 8:12-13)*

[12]*"**Then the fourth angel sounded:** And a third of the sun was struck, a third of the moon, and a third of the stars, so that a third of them were darkened. A third of the day did not shine, and likewise the night. [13]And I looked, and I heard an angel flying through the midst of heaven, saying with a loud voice, "Woe, woe, woe to the inhabitants of the Earth, because of the remaining blasts of the trumpet of the three angels who are about to sound!"*

Fifth Trumpet: *(First "woe") The Locusts from the Bottomless Pit (Revelation 9:1-12)*

[1]*"Then **the fifth angel sounded:** And I saw a star fallen from heaven to the earth. To him was given the key to the bottomless pit [2] and he opened the bottomless pit, and smoke arose out of the*

pit like the smoke of a great furnace. So the sun and the air were darkened because of the smoke of the pit. [3] Then out of the smoke locusts came upon the earth. And to them was given power, as the scorpions of the earth have power. [4]They were commanded not to harm the grass of the earth, or any green thing, or any tree, but only those men who do not have the seal of God on their foreheads. [5]And they were not given authority to kill them, but to torment them for **five months**. Their torment was like the torment of a scorpion when it strikes a man. [6] In those days men will seek death and will not find it; they will desire to die, and death will flee from them. [7]The shape of the locusts was like horses prepared for battle. On their heads were crowns of something like gold, and their faces were like the faces of men. [8]They had hair like women's hair, and their teeth were like lions' teeth. [9]And they had breastplates like breastplates of iron, and the sound of their wings was like the sound of chariots with many horses running into battle. [10]They had tails like scorpions, and there were stings in their tails. Their power was to hurt men **five months**. [11]And they had as King over them the Angle of the bottomless pit whose name in Hebrew is Abaddon, but in Greek he has the name Apollyon [12]one *woe is past. Behold, still two more woes are coming after these things".*

Sixth Trumpet: *(Second "woe") The Angles from the Euphratus (Revelation 9:13-21)*

> [13] *"Then **the sixth angel sounded:** And I heard a voice from the four horns of the golden altar which is before God, [14]saying to the sixth angel who had the trumpet, "Release the four angels who are bound at the great river Euphrates." [15]So the four angels, who had been pre-pared for the hour and day and month and year, were released to kill a third of mankind. [16]Now the number of the army of the horsemen was two hundred million; I heard the number of them. [17] And thus I saw the horses in the vision: those who sat on them had breastplates of fiery red, hyacinth blue, and sulfur yellow; and the heads of the horses were like the heads of lions; and out of their mouths came fire, smoke, and brimstone. [18]By these three plagues a third of man-kind was killed—by the fire and the smoke and the brimstone which came out of their mouths. [19]For their power is in their mouth and in their tails; for their tails are like serpents, having heads; and with them they do harm. [20]But the rest of mankind, who were not killed by these plagues, **did not repent***

of the works of their hands, that they should not worship demons, and idols of gold, silver, brass, stone, and wood, which can neither see nor hear nor walk. [21]And they did not repent of their murders or their sorceries or their sexual immorality or their thefts.

Seventh Trumpet: *(Third "woe") The Kingdom Proclaimed (Revelation 11:15-19)*

*"[15] Then **the seventh angel sounded:** And there were loud voices in heaven, saying, "The kingdoms of this world have become the kingdoms of our Lord and of His Christ, and He shall reign forever and ever!" [16] And the twenty-four elders who sat before God on their thrones fell on their faces and worshiped God, [17] saying:*

> *"We give You thanks, O Lord God Almighty,
> The One who is and who was and who is to come,
> Because You have taken Your great power and reigned.
> [18] The nations were angry, and Your wrath has come,
> And the time of the dead, that they should be judged,
> And that You should reward Your servants the prophets and*

the saints,
And those who fear Your name,
small and great,
And should destroy those who
destroy the earth."

[19] *Then the temple of God was opened in heaven, and the ark of His covenant was seen in His temple. And there were lightnings, noises, thunderings, an earthquake, and great hail."*

Please make note, that during the blowing of Trumpet Five, the woe of flying locust like scorpions, that it says in Revelation 9, verse 5 and 10 that the plague will last for five months and in verse 6, that those tormented will try to die but cannot, death will flee from them.

The Bowls come next in Revelation 16:1-21 (these also occur during the seven years of Great Tribulation), [1] *"Then I heard a loud voice from the temple saying to the seven angels, "Go and pour out the bowls of the wrath of God on the earth."*

Part 12

The Bowls

God's wrath poured out on the earth as we read; Revelation 16:1: *[1]"Then I heard a loud voice from the temple saying to the seven angels, "Go and pour out the bowls of the wrath of God on the earth."*

First Bowl: *Malignant Sores (Revelation 16:2)*

> *[2]"So the first went and poured out his bowl upon the earth, and a foul and loathsome sore came upon the men who had the mark of the beast and those who worshiped his image."*

Second Bowl: *The Sea Turns to Blood (Revelation 16:3)*

> *[3]"Then the second angel poured out his bowl on the sea, and it became blood as of a dead man; and every living creature in the sea died."*

Third Bowl: *The Waters Turn to Blood (Revelation 16:4-7)*

> *[4]"Then the third angel poured out his bowl on the rivers and springs of water,*

and they became blood. ⁵And I heard the angel of the waters saying: "You are righteous, O Lord, The One who is and who was and who is to be," Because You have judged these things. ⁶For they have shed the blood of saints and prophets, and You have given them blood to drink. For it is their just due." ⁷And I heard another from the altar saying, "Even so, Lord God Almighty, true and righteous are Your judgments."

Fourth Bowl: *Men Are Scorched (Revelation 16:8,9*

⁸"Then the fourth angel poured out his bowl on the sun, and power was given to him to scorch men with fire. ⁹And men were scorched with great heat, and they blasphemed the name of God who has power over these plagues; **and they did not repent** *and give Him glory."*

Fifth Bowl: *Darkness and Pain (Revelation 16:10-11)*

¹⁰"Then the fifth angel poured out his bowl on the throne of the beast, and his kingdom became full of darkness; and they gnawed their tongues because of the pain. ¹¹They blasphemed the God of Heaven because of their pains and their sores, **and did not repent of their deeds".**

Sixth Bowl: *Euphrates Dried Up. (Revelation 16: 12-16)*

74

[12] "Then the sixth angel poured out his bowl on the great river Euphrates, and its water was dried up, so that the way of the kings from the east might be prepared. [13]And I saw three unclean spirits like frogs coming out of the mouth of the dragon, out of the mouth of the beast, and out of the mouth of the false prophet. [14]For they are spirits of demons, performing signs, which go out to the kings of the Earth and of the whole world, to gather them to the battle of that great day of God Almighty. (Jesus speaking) [15]"Behold, I am coming as a thief. Blessed is he who watches, and keeps his garments, lest he walk naked and they see his shame." [16]And they gathered them together to the place called in Hebrew, Armageddon."

Seventh Bowl: *The Earth Utterly Shaken (Revelation 16: 17-21)*

[17] "Then the seventh angel poured out his bowl into the air, and a loud voice came out of the temple of Heaven, from the throne, saying, "It is done!" [18]And there were noises and thunderings and lightnings; and there was a great earthquake (shaking), such a mighty and great earthquake (a most violent shaking of all time) as had not occurred since men were on the earth. [19]Now the

great city was divided into three parts, and the cities of the nations fell. And great Babylon was remembered before God, to give her the cup of the wine of the fierceness of His wrath. [20]*Then every island fled away (disappeared), and the mountains were not found (disappeared).* [21]*And great hail from heaven fell upon men, each hailstone about the weight of a talent (75 lbs.). Men blasphemed God because of the plague of the hail, since that plague was exceedingly great."* (There was no covering, nothing left standing after the most powerful of all shakings of earth).

Part 13

My Conclusion

N ow the book of Revelation (or at least Chapters 5-16) reveals God's mercy, His love, His intense wrath, and where mankind is living in this present time within the book of Revelation. Now, Revelation has meaning because it shows where the twenty-first century people are positioned and what all of mankind will soon experience **within the next few years**.

So the question is: Do you believe the Bible? God in His mercy has not left us as believers, sitting and waiting for some unknown event at some unknown point in time. Nor has He left the non believers without seeing His Mercy clearly revealed before them one more time. No, the Lord has said, presently we are waiting for the fulfillment of a total number of martyrs to die and when that number (that God has set) is reached, then Jesus will open the "sixth seal" and everyone alive on the earth will know that the wrath of God has come to the ungodly people of the world, to judge and avenge the martyrs' blood on the ungodly who dwell on the earth (Revelation 6:10, The fifth seal [10] *And they cried with a loud voice, saying, "How long, O Lord, holy and true, until You judge and avenge our blood on those who dwell on the earth?"*).

If you are one of the many billions of people alive today who is definitely a non-believing individual (a person who does not believe that Jesus Christ is the only Son of God, savior of all humanity, who came to earth, was born of a virgin, grew up a sinless man, who died a tortuous, humiliating death on an old rugged cross, to set at liberty, all mankind who are bound by sin on their way to eternal damnation in the flames of hell), then pay attention because no matter what your status or position is in this life, your remaining days of status quo are numbered.

If you make it through the great earthquake or the violent devastating shaking of the planet alive (the sixth seal, Revelation 6:12-17: *Sixth Seal: Cosmic Disturbances* *12 I looked when He opened the sixth seal, and behold, there was a great earthquake; and the sun became black as sackcloth of hair, and the moon became like blood. 13 And the stars of heaven fell to the earth, as a fig tree drops its late figs when it is shaken by a mighty wind. 14 Then the sky receded as a scroll when it is rolled up, and every mountain and island was moved out of its place. 15 And the kings of the earth, the great men, the rich men, the commanders, the mighty men, every slave and every free man, hid themselves in the caves and in the rocks of the mountains, 16 and said to the mountains and rocks, "Fall on us and hide us from the face of Him who sits on the throne and from the wrath of the Lamb! 17 For the great day of His wrath has come, and who is able to stand?"),* then you will experience the last worldwide sweeping opportunity to receive Jesus Christ as your Savior and Lord. You may not be a Christian now as you read this, but I hope and pray you can see how much God loves you by giving you one last chance to be washed by the blood and receive Jesus Christ into your heart prior to the rapture (or catching away) of all believers.

This last end-time revival or conversion of unbelievers will be the greatest soul-winning harvest that the world has ever known. There will be hundreds of millions of people saved from their sins or born-again during a five to seven day period and then all living Christians will be caught up (raptured) to meet Jesus Christ in the clouds. The Christians are caught up at that time, because life on planet earth is going to turn nasty and violent as the masses become like a hungry pack of wolves trying to satisfy their personal needs for food and water to survive. It will become a time of "survival of the fittest" which means the man with the biggest gun and the most bullets will be left standing. For the next few months, life on earth will be extremely hard and cruel, until Marshall Law is restored in major cities around the world. I feel sorry for anyone who lets the "Great Revival" pass them by because of their hardened heart and disbelief.

If you are reading this book as a born-again believer, secure as many copies as you can and pass them out to each local family in your community. This will help people not to be caught by surprise when the sixth seal is opened and the great shake occurs and life on earth instantly becomes dark and grim.

I encourage all believers to begin praying for the events that are coming in the near future. Now, you might ask, "How do we know what to pray for?" That's a fair question and my answer is, you don't, but the Holy Spirit does. The Holy Spirit knows every detail of what you should pray for and what you should pray about, so let Him pray through you. (See Part 14, about praying in spirit.)

If you have read this book as a non-believer, I have three words to share with you: repent, repent, and repent. Let Jesus Christ become your Savior and Lord today. The Bible says, *"Believe on the Lord Jesus Christ and you will be saved"* (Acts 16:31), then confess it with your mouth.

This book is not written with any intent to make a profit; any book sales or love offerings that come in will be used to print additional copies to put into the hands of people. Please remember the count of Christian Martyrs could be fulfilled at any time and then Jesus will open the six seal, so be prepared. Jesus said, *"What I say to you, I say to all : Watch !"* (Mark 13:37)

To those who say they have plenty of time, *"³ For when they say, "Peace and safety!" then sudden destruction comes upon them, as labor pains upon a pregnant woman. And they shall not escape."* *(1 Thessalonians 5:3)*

May the Lord bless you and keep you until His coming. To God be the glory, great things He has done.

The final part 14 is so very important for all Christians alive today. In the days ahead each believer needs the power and authority of God's Gift to each believer, operating in his or her life. This is not an option, it's a must and it is available for you as a gift from God, so just simply receive the gift. The Baptism of The Holy Ghost, The Promise of The Father.

Part 14

Praying the Will of the Father

Every believer should realize, for whatever amount of time remains before the opening of the sixth seal, he or she needs to walk in the power of the Holy Spirit because Satan, our worst enemy, will be trying harder than ever to tear every Christian apart over this remaining time period. If you, as a Christian, have NOT been baptised in the Holy Ghost with the sign of prayer and praise in tongues, then you are a soldier standing naked on the battleground.

All Christians baptised in the Holy Ghost are now dressed in the whole armor of God according to Ephesians 6:11-18:

> *"11 Put on the whole armor of God, that you may be able to stand against the wiles of the devil. 12 For we do not wrestle against flesh and blood, but against principalities, against powers, against the rulers of the darkness of this age, against spiritual hosts of wickedness in the heavenly places. 13 Therefore take up the whole armor of God, that*

you may be able to withstand in the evil day, and having done all, to stand.

[14] Stand therefore, having girded your waist with truth, having put on the breastplate of righteousness, [15] and having shod your feet with the preparation of the gospel of peace; [16] above all, taking the shield of faith with which you will be able to quench all the fiery darts of the wicked one. [17] And take the helmet of salvation, and the sword of the Spirit, which is the word of God; **[18] praying always** *with all prayer and* **supplication in the Spirit**, *being watchful to this end with all perseverance and supplication for all the saints"*

Let's focus for a moment on verse eighteen, which says: *"Praying always with all prayer and supplication in the Spirit, being watchful to this end with all perseverance and supplication for all the saints."* Pay attention and notice the words: ***"praying always** with all prayer and supplication **in the Spirit."*** (Verse 18).

Other verses that come to mind in 1 Thessalonians 5:16-18 *[16]"Rejoice always, [17]pray without ceasing, [18]in everything give thanks; for this is the will of God in Christ Jesus for you."* Pay attention to verse 17, "pray without ceasing".

The phrases *"praying always"* and *"pray without ceasing"* are the same thing, but how does one accomplish these directives? I think everyone would agree it is not possible to pray all the time or non-stop. I think what is being said, is we Christians should pray as much as we can or as often as is possible throughout all the remaining days that we live and for our prayers to be the most effective, we should follow the biblical example and pray in the Spirit in our own private prayer time.

When a believer prays in the Holy Ghost (or in the Spirit) in his or her prayer language, this is the time of improving yourself spiritually, when one yields the heart, mind and tongue to the Holy Spirit to pray **the perfect will of God**. In 1 Corinthians 14:2 it says, *"For he who speaks (prays) in a tongue does not speak to men but to God, for no one understands him; however, in the spirit he speaks mysteries."* Your mind has nothing to do with the sounds you are praying. In 1 Corinthians 14:14, it says: *"For if I pray in a tongue, my spirit prays, but my understanding is unfruitful."* Praise God, you don't have to think about what you are praying, because it is not you praying; it is the Holy Ghost praying through you. This is the ultimate prayer of faith, allowing the Holy Spirit to pray through you, knowing that He knows every need in the world in total detail.

Remember, the Holy Ghost is God in you. *"The Baptism of the Holy Ghost is God's gift to every believer (salvation is God's gift to every sinner)."* God, your Heavenly Father, wants you to use your gift of prayer as often as you can. In 1 Thessalonians 5:17 it says: *"pray without ceasing"* or as much as you can. Your brain could not continue for long periods of time, praying in your native tongue out of your physical mind. Before long, you would start to repeat yourself or you would not know what else to pray. However, that is not the case when praying in the Holy Ghost. You can continue to pray the will of God in the Spirit as long as you are physically able. *"As you pray in the Spirit, it edifies you"* (1 Corinthians 14:4) or builds you up. I once went to an all night prayer meeting at church, where we prayed in the Spirit from eight p.m. to eight a.m. (twelve hours) and I felt more refreshed when I left than when I started. You can take a break and then continue right on, because the Holy Ghost does not forget where He stopped.

The baptism of the Holy Ghost with the gift of speaking or praying in tongues has been so important and necessary, ever since The Day of Pentecost. Paul made it clear in I Corinthians 14:18. He said: *"I thank my God I speak with tongues more than you all."*

It was important back then and I believe it to be more important for us today. We are living at a super fast pace in these days of the twenty-first century. God the Father knew from the foundation of time that believers would need a more expeditious, more effective way to pray, than by using our limited minds. Think about it: someone comes up to you and asks you to pray for a problem they are entangled with, and they even go into a lot of detail about the problem (generally more that they need to), and after they leave, numerous questions came to you about their situation. However, you remember the Holy Ghost knows every detail about every situation in the world, in every person's life and He knows exactly how to pray the effectual fervent prayer (the will of the Father) that avails much (James 5:16): *"Confess your trespasses to one another, and pray for one another, that you may be healed. The effective, fervent prayer of a righteous man avails much."*

Over any and every situation or problem, even if you are earnestly praying over one of your own children, there is no way you can begin to know every detail about what you need to pray about, but thank God, the Holy Ghost knows *every detail* about the matter and how to pray specifically for the best results.

Here is a side note, the Holy Ghost shared with me about *"Praying In Tongues"*. The sounds that flow out of your mouth when you are praying in the Holy Ghost are *"spiritually compressed"*; meaning a small portion of any sound coming out of your inner most being can represent ten thousand words in any native tongue. This is God, the Holy Ghost, praying to God, the Heavenly Father, through to God the Son, Jesus Christ, our intercessor. So, now you can clearly see that praying an hour in the Holy Ghost is much more effective than praying an hour using your mind. God knew from the beginning of time things would have to change with time. Not God, for we have and unchanging God. We did receive a new covenant, the blood of lambs would no longer do, so God sent His only begotten Son into the world to shed His blood at Calvary as a one time, final blood sacrifice for the forgiveness of sins and we must go in through Jesus Christ to get to the Father. Thank you Jesus! So, at Pentecost, the time was right to receive the "Promise of the Father" (Luke 24:49: *49 Behold, I send the Promise of My Father upon you; but tarry in the city of Jerusalem until you are endued with power from on high."* and Acts 1:4: *4 And being assembled together with them, He commanded them not to depart from Jerusalem, but to wait for the Promise of the Father, "which," He said, "you have heard from Me"*), so every believer, henceforth, that would be baptized with the

Holy Ghost with the evidence of speaking in tongues, would be filled with *power*; power over all the forces of hell. Praise God; they needed it then and oh Lord, we do need it now! For then and now, Satan wages war against every believer as declared in Ephesians 6:10-12:

> *"**The Whole Armor of God** [10] Finally, my brethren, be strong in the Lord and in the power of His might. [11] Put on the whole armor of God, that you may be able to stand against the wiles of the devil. [12] For we do not wrestle against flesh and blood, but against principalities, against powers, against the rulers of the darkness of this age, against spiritual hosts of wickedness in the heavenly places."*

I'm sorry to say, over the years, the battle has intensified and will continue to do so. We should thank God for the gift of the Holy Ghost and the gift of praying in the Spirit and all other special gifts.

One final thought about praying in the Spirit, since it originates from the Holy Spirit and it is He who is praying through you, Satan cannot understand a single word of the prayer because he doesn't have the mind of Christ.

Now, you might think praying in the Spirit sounds like a wonderful gift, but you don't have it, so how does one receive this gift?

Well, if you remember how easy it was to get saved, you are halfway there because that is the only requirement to be baptized in the Holy Ghost: you must be saved. Since it's a gift from God, then in faith, lift up your hands toward heaven and tell your Heavenly Father you are ready to receive His Gift as promised, so receive the Baptism in the Holy Ghost right now, in Jesus' name. Amen !

By faith, you received the Lord's gift of the Holy Ghost and you will speak in tongues, then you can pray in the Spirit as often as possible.

The second thing you are blessed with when you receive the Baptism in the Holy Ghost is you fall deeper in love with Jesus. At one time, some referred to the event as "the baptism of love" because of the deeper love relationship with Jesus Christ.

If you are a Christian (born-again), you need and should want "The Baptism in the Holy Spirit" so your prayer time can be more effective, more powerful, more refreshing, and more meaningful; knowing the Holy Spirit can cover every situation, circumstance, need, sickness around the world for every human being who needs prayer.

Praise God, what a wonderful gift that God has made available to every believer. Jesus said: *"Ask and it will be given to you"* (Matthew 7:7)

Reference scripture, to the baptism in the Holy Spirit:

> **Acts 1:4-5:** *The Holy Spirit Promised*
> *⁴"And being assembled together with them, He commanded them not to depart from Jerusalem, but to wait for the Promise of the Father, "which," He said, "you have heard from Me; ⁵ for John truly baptized with water, but you*

shall be baptized with the Holy Spirit not many days from now."

Acts 1:8 *⁸ But you shall receive power when the Holy Spirit has come upon you; and you shall be witnesses to Me in Jerusalem, and in all Judea and Samaria, and to the end of the earth."*

Acts 9:17 *"¹⁷ And Ananias went his way and entered the house; and laying his hands on him he said, "Brother Saul, the Lord Jesus, who appeared to you on the road as you came, has sent me that you may receive your sight and be filled with the Holy Spirit."*

Acts 2:1-4: Coming of the Holy Spirit
"¹ When the Day of Pentecost had fully come, they were all with one accord in one place. ² And suddenly there came a sound from heaven, as of a rushing mighty wind, and it filled the whole house where they were sitting. ³ Then there appeared to them divided tongues, as of fire, and one sat upon each of them. ⁴ And they were all filled with the Holy Spirit and began to speak with other tongues, as the Spirit gave them utterance."

Acts 10:44-46: *The Holy Spirit Falls on the Gentiles "⁴⁴ While Peter was still* *speaking these words, the Holy Spirit fell upon all those who heard the word. [45] And those of the circumcision who believed were astonished, as many as came with Peter, because the gift of the Holy Spirit had been poured out on the Gentiles also. [46] For they heard them speak with tongues and magnify God."*

Acts 2:17: *[17] 'And it shall come to pass in the last days, says God,*
That I will pour out of My Spirit on all flesh;
Your sons and your daughters shall prophesy,
Your young men shall see visions,
Your old men shall dream dreams."

Acts 19:5: *"[5] When they heard this, they were baptized in the name of the Lord Jesus."*

Acts 8:14-17: *The Sorcerer's Sin "[14] Now when the apostles who were at Jerusalem heard that Samaria had received the word of God, they sent Peter and John to them, [15] who, when they had come down, prayed for them that they might receive the Holy Spirit. [16] For as yet He had fallen upon none of them. They had only been baptized in the name of the Lord Jesus. [17] Then they* *laid hands on them, and they received the Holy Spirit."*

BIBLIOGRAPHY

1. The New King James Version, Thomas Nelson Publishers, Nashville, TN, 1988.
2. Casey, John L. Upheaval, TRAFFORD Publishing, 2016.
3. Lowe, David W. Earthquake Resurrection, 2005.

About the Author

Paul T. Klumpp

My life, as a young boy, who was born in Corpus, Christi, Texas, in the early 1940s, was not much different than most boys of that day and time, except that my parents owned a grocery store and that was different for me. I got a treat each day when I arrived home from school. My treat was either a Grapette soda or an ice cream bar. In those days that was very special. The most important event of my boyhood days happened when I was 8 years old, on a typical Sunday morning in a small town Nazarene Church, the Love of Jesus Christ touched my heart and I went to the front of the church, knelt at the altar and gave my heart to Jesus Christ and I was "Born Again" in 1951. I now had a new friend Jesus Christ, who was always with me, to lead me on the path of righteousness for His Name sake. He said "I'll lead, you follow!" sounds simple enough and it is, except now, I had gained an enemy with a passion to kill me. His name is Satan.

So through the years of junior high and high school, the battle of good and evil was fought daily over who I would follow. The Truth or the deceiver of truth (who most often looks and sounds like the Truth). When you are a teenager trying to create a manly (fleshly) image for yourself, the walk is extremely tough at this time because your advisory, the devil, is now saying everything is cool and his way is the only way to have fun and to be popular.

The teenage years were the worst years of my life spiritually but I had Godly parents that knew how to call on Jesus and they kept me in church. I don't know how many times I fell and started over but Jesus never said anything about it. He just put His arms around me and told me how much He loved me. Then a song would flood into my heart that told my story which was "I was sinking deep in sin, far from the peaceful shore, very deeply stained within, sinking to rise no more. But the Master of the sea heard my despairing cry, from the waters lifted me; Now safe am I. When nothing else could help, Love lifted me."

As does happen with most teenagers, they finally grow up (PRAISE GOD) and became responsible adult men and women. Well, that's what happened to me. At age 24, my heart was struck one Sunday evening as I entered church, by a sweet young lady, whose name was Connie, whom I had known and attended church with Connie and her family for years. Connie had just graduated from High School and my lights finally went on and we were married one year later, July 2, 1966 and remained happily married for 47 years when on September 4, 2013 Connie passed and went home to be with Jesus, a most sad and difficult parting for me, my two children and their families.

Back in 1980, the Lord helped me start a High Tech Business serving refineries, chemical plants and power plants around the world. My travels presented numerous opportunities to share The Gospel of The

Lord Jesus Christ and to meet new Christians in various countries. Praise God! Here I am, in 2017, still providing unique design and troubleshooting services to several original/new clients and still sharing the Love and Joy of Jesus Christ.

During my college years (1962 to 1968), the Holy Ghost put an interest in my spirit for the Book of Revelation, the last book of the New Testament. I did not understand why but I began to read it. After reading it through several times, I noticed that I had no more understanding of what I was reading than when I first read it. So I got frustrated and quit reading it for a while. After a couple of years went by, I once again opened my Bible and read Revelation 1:1-2, *"The Revelation of Jesus Christ, which God gave Him to show His servants, things which must shortly take place and He sent and signified it by His angel to His servant John, who bore witness to the Word of God and to the testimony of Jesus Christ, to all things that he saw."* Continuing on, I started again reading the Book of Revelation.

I wanted to know what the Book of Revelation had to say to people of my time, approaching the start of the twenty first century. Is the book's message just futuristic? You know, so far out in the future that we don't need to even read it today.

The Holy Spirit began showing me that we have actually been living in the "seals" of Revelation (Chapter 6) since Jesus left the earth about 2,000 years ago, at least the first five seals.

Since 1951, when I accepted Jesus Christ as my savior, I have been trying to serve the Lord and bring Glory and Honor to His Name. I have made mistakes, I have fallen flat on my face in doing what I thought was right. If I had it to do over again, would I do some things differently to avoid hurting some people? Yes, I would. You see, when you hurt people, more importantly you also hurt Jesus, saying you're sorry and asking for forgiveness is not easy but it is necessary. Jesus made a point in Matthew 25:31-46 concerning offending others as being the same as offending Him. Yes I have fallen many times but Jesus tells me "Don't ever give up" and I won't for there is not another road to walk, that leads Home, to Heaven.

Life is about doing your best to please God, by the power and direction of The Holy Ghost who lives in us to help us every step of the way, as we walk the road of Righteousness that leads us to Heaven.

Praise God! Jesus is The Way, The Truth and The Life. It is only through Him and what He did at Calvary, giving His Life to redeem us from Sin, giving each person an opportunity to be made free from the bondage of sin and death. THANK YOU JESUS, for making me free.

CPSIA information can be obtained
at www.ICGtesting.com
Printed in the USA
LVHW082302160419
614446LV00040B/796/P